AF263283

when I believed in love

a. e. urban

when I believed in love
A. E. Urban

Cover photo taken by Sarah Williamson of Together We Click
togetherweclick.com
Instagram: @togetherweclick

Cover design by Arianna Urban

Page Art

© Naufa
© Zern Liew
© A3701027
© Simple Line
© ESA
© Riz
© Valenty
© Luckystep
© Mazaya
© Mitay20
© KY
© ngudakarti
© Matias
© Garkushart
© samuii
© Anna
© inna72
© Maria

for everyone who has ever loved with all they had
who have weathered the storm of heartache
for those who still believe in love
even when it left them behind

those nights
that you're consumed by grief
when you ache to the core of your bones
no one comes to save you
you gasp for air between tears
that fall harder than rain
you beg the universe to take it back
to bring them back
you feel weak for wanting something
someone
so bad
it's like part of you is missing
you'll never get it back
love like that strikes like lightning
never twice in the same place
on those nights
you're brave
for loving so fiercely
that you opened your heart that much
that it could hurt so bad
you risked it all anyway
when you believed in love

part one

it started with pancakes

He rode past her on an old bike with rusty red paint, as she gazed at the dusty titles in the bookstore window. It was half a block before he decided to turn around.

"Hey," he said with a smile. She turned her forest green eyes to him and raised an eyebrow, his breath caught in his chest.

"Hi there," she said smirking, crossing her arms as she stood under the awning of an antique store.

"Are you from around here?" he asked as he pulled the bike up next to the curb. He noticed that she had a slight sunburn and the hat she wore hid fiery red waves spilling down her back.

"No, actually, I'm visiting a friend for a few days."

"I hope you're enjoying your visit so far."
She studied him carefully before answering. He had a strong jaw that boasted some light stubble, sandy blonde hair, messy, but not unkempt. A little rough around the edges but seemed nice enough. She started walking again, swaying with the breeze as she spoke, he followed along, walking with the bike.

"It's been great, this is one of my favorite places to be," he smiled again and she couldn't help but smile back.

"Do you want to get some breakfast?"
She laughed, unsure of what to make of him.

"Do you always ask strangers out for breakfast when you meet them?" she asked.

"Not all of them, only beautiful ones, from out of town," she blushed.
He was charming and handsome, she had to admit. What could breakfast hurt?

"You do realize it's 2 o'clock in the afternoon, not exactly prime breakfast time."

"Oh, it's the perfect time for breakfast," he said, pushing the bike up on the sidewalk to a rack, and locking it into place.

"So, what do you say? Pancakes?"
She shrugged, "I suppose there's no harm in pancakes, I'm Anna, by the way."

"Parker," he said.
He took her outstretched hand and shook it lightly.

I felt it
        as soon as you walked in
                shared glances across the room

I think you knew it too
        by the way gravity
                pulled me to you

this was how our story
        would begin

this could be the start of something new
buzzing in my veins when I think of you
hold my hand in the middle of the street
I could move to the way your *heart* beats

arriving in a *golden* glow
unlike anything I've ever known
you showed me the way
back to myself in twinkling light rays

meet me where the stars
disappear into the horizon

hold me in your arms
as twilight *intertwines* us

the dress I wore
the night you *swore*
that you would never leave

the way we danced
in kitchen light
I never will forget

wind whipped through my hair
holding hands we drove back roads
getting *lost* with you

maybe it's the way your eyes shimmered
in the moonlight
or the way your laughter filled the emptiness
within her *tired* soul

maybe she needed a wild new adventure
or for you to keep smiling at her

whatever it was
she wanted to stay lost in the moment
until the stars rained down around you

the way our eyes meet
breathless as you move closer
surrender to me

"Don't kiss me unless you mean it,"
I sighed as you brushed the hair from my face.

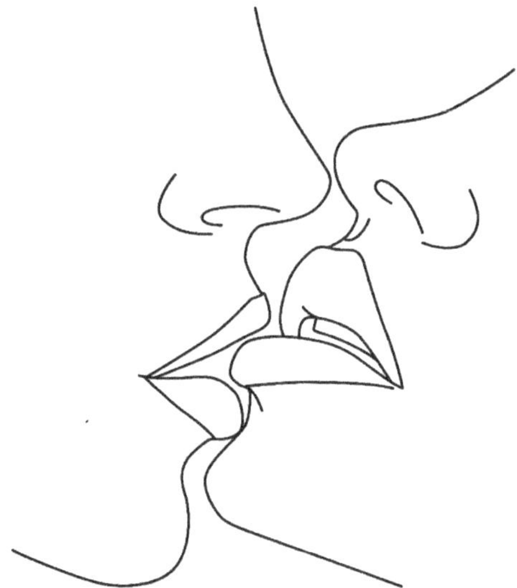

it was a first kiss
a slow motion *blur*
an ember to flame
a moment of bliss

slip your hand into mine
        anywhere you lead I'll go
with you by my side
        unafraid of the unknown

I want to

  f
   a
   l
    l

madly
passionately
wildly
in love

the kind of love
that makes the sun feel warmer
the stars shine brighter
the weight of the world feel lighter

the kind of love
that makes poets blush
whiskey taste sweeter

the kind of love
that *stays*

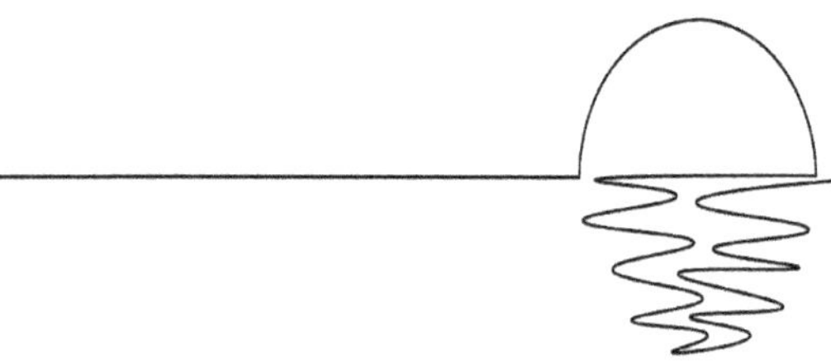

you stood inches from me
in the middle of the street
under an orange streaked sky
as we kissed

everything melted away
as if in those 20 seconds
you could erase every scar
mend every broken piece
found etched within my heart
you pulled back to look at me

with *fire* in your eyes
I knew I never wanted
to reflect as anything less
than sparks in the setting sun

hoping the universe
is finally on my side
although fate has never been kind

I never want to forget
how your lips *crush* mine
the sound of your laughter
as the world sleeps around us
lost in our own time

she sees the way the stars glow in his eyes
        gold specks of stardust *explode* from the sky
green and blue like the deepest sea
        there's no place she'd rather be

familiar like the worn pages of an old book
        all it took was one look
she fell before she even had a chance
        no turning back locked in his trance

waiting patiently
the days drag on forever
won't you come *save* me

remember that night that we got *high*
laid in bed looking out at the sky
1 a.m. and I wanted to say it then

"What are you afraid of?" he asked, holding his hand out.
He pulled her to her feet and she looked deep into his blue eyes.
"That I'll never feel this way again."

smiling at everything and nothing
the sun washes over my skin
I feel the glow from the inside
finally there's *peace* in my heart

it's that
stay up all night
butterflies in your stomach
can't stop *smiling*
buzzing in your head
makes you drunk
kind of feeling

    it's that
    stumble in the dark kissing
    laughing as you collapse
    waking up to see them sleep
    pulling them closer
    hearts *beating* as one
    kind of feeling

        it's that
        stay forever
        hand in mine
        fall in love for the last time
        kind of *feeling*

part two

stay

She woke as the soft morning light shone through the window, still wrapped in his arms, everything felt like a dream. As he breathed in comfortable sleep next to her, she thought about everything that had brought her to this moment. Six days had passed since she'd had the best blueberry pancakes she had ever tasted. As often as she had been to Cardinal Hill, she'd never been to the small town on the other side of the island.

Letting out a sigh, Parker shifted and she turned to face him. She studied the splattering of freckles that were painted across his nose brought on by the sun, she ran a finger over the stubble that scratched her when they kissed. He opened his eyes and smiled.

"Good morning," he pulled her closer and kissed her nose.

"Morning," she smiled.

He pulled the blankets up around them, as she laid her head on his chest, he stroked her hair. They hadn't really talked about it, but she bit her lip thinking about her flight home in two days. *Two days*, she let out a sigh.

"Where'd you go?" he asked.

She shook her head.

"Nowhere, I need a shower... and coffee," she said, rolling off of him to sit on the side of the bed.

"You shower, I'll make coffee," he said, kissing her before he made his way down the little spiral staircase that led to a small landing next to the kitchen. She picked her phone up off the side table, scrolled through email notifications, news, and missed texts. As she padded into the bathroom, she turned on one of her favorite playlists, pulled the hair tie from her wrist, and tied her hair up in a loose bun. She could hear the soft clatter of pans, smiling as she turned the water on and stepped in.

...

"Feel better?" he asked as she came down the stairs, handing her a cup of coffee.

"Mhm," she took a sip and sat down at the table.

"You were thinking about leaving earlier, weren't you?"
She didn't meet his gaze but shook her head yes.

"It's only two days," she said quietly.

"Stay."
She looked up at him, brow furrowed as if she didn't hear him right.

"What?" she whispered.

"Stay," he said, moving to kneel in front of her.

"Don't go home yet. There's some short term studios you can rent, or you can stay here with me. I just don't want you to go." he trailed off, the urgency in his voice was something unexpected.
She reached out and put her hand on his face, not sure what to say, until the words tumbled out.

"I love you."

lay here with me
under the hazy sky
forget the world around us
not ready to say *goodbye*

follow me through the *dark*
hold me when I fall apart
tell me it will be all right
stay longer than the rest

I woke to the golden glow
        of sunlight across my skin
tangled in blankets with you
        a place to call my own

tell me your *truths*
I'll kiss them
gently from your lips
sparks showering the night
as we collide

waiting in the quiet
you *whisper* my name

shivers down my spine
when your lips find mine

I don't know how I didn't see
you were right here in front of me

I'd pick you
on any sleepless night
even when you're right
in every song
in every mood

I'd pick you
for endless laughter
happily ever after
in every fight
in every kiss

I'd pick you

a rare kind of love
a safe place to sleep
a phone call away
to say it will be okay
words you can believe
kisses found in the dark
feels like forever

rough hands on soft skin
the sound of wanting you more
fumbling in the dark

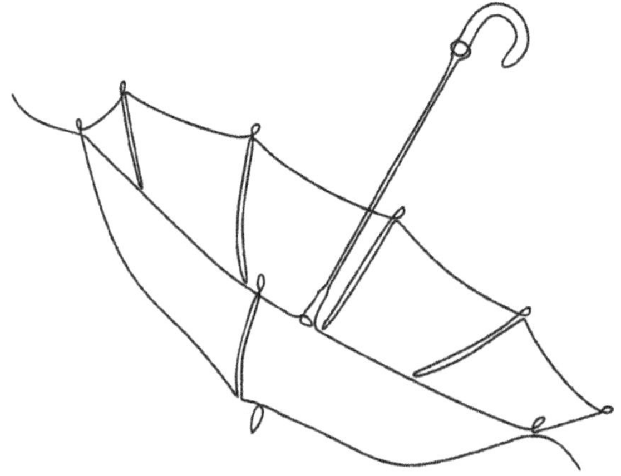

she wanted to say that she knew
all the quirks about him
how he brushed his teeth
what he smelled like after he shaved
the things he liked in his smoothies
that he hated the rain
how he stayed up to hear the frogs
sing to the sky in the middle of the night
the way he looked her in the eyes
when they were in a fight to say *sorry*
those were her favorite things
that the world didn't know about
how he held her until she fell asleep
even when he wasn't tired
he played her favorite songs
so she could sing in the car
taught her how to love
all her flawed broken parts
on the darkest days
she loved how he loved her
the way no one else would

I know your house
like the back of my hand
a map of the places we've kissed
my things on the nightstand
remember that night
I got too high
counted my footsteps in the dark
up the stairs to sleep by your side
we watched the sun rise through the trees
nothing could come between

you & me

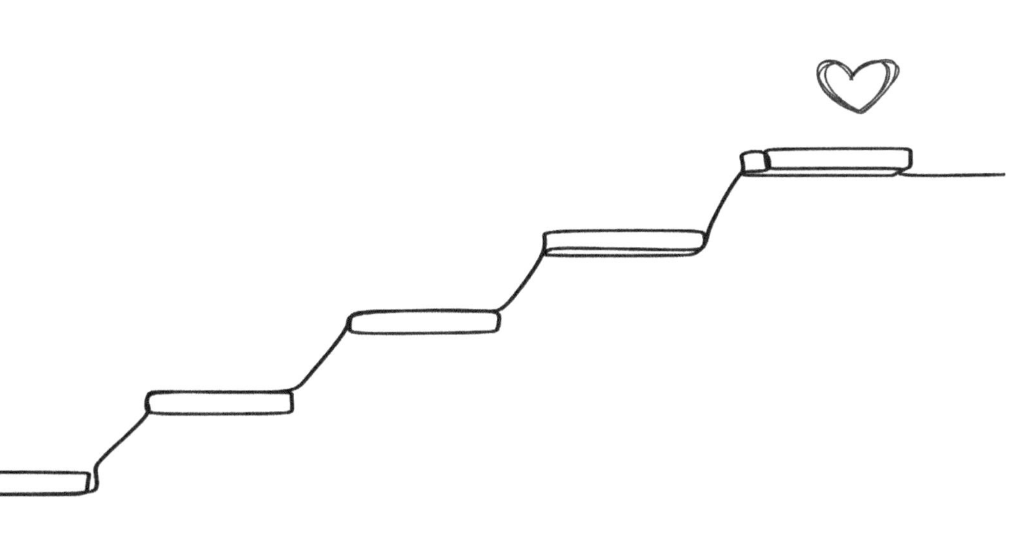

dancing to the sound of thunder
under the spotlight of the moon
we spun as the world stood still
your hands on my hips
you don't know how it feels
when you touch me
fire in my veins
never giving you up

laughing in the summer breeze
chasing all my *wildest* dreams
they all lead back to you

take my hand
hold me close
move to the sound
of rain on the roof
we could be
the living *proof*
of happily ever after
in a world
to stubborn to love

stay with me forever
spoken softly in the dark
candle lit *promises*

happiness painted in shades of you
you could say it's almost blue
the way the summer sky
saw so much of us
talk of forever

never would have known
with you asleep beside me
how it feels like *home*

I saved you a spot
on the empty pillow next to me
the side where the moon shines
through the cracks in the blinds
as the blankets reach
to consume us in warmth
drifting into soundless sleep
your fingers *intertwine* with mine

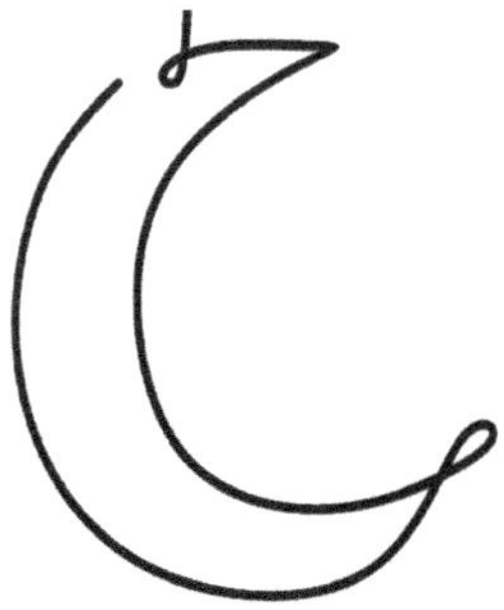

with him
it was *magic*

wrap me into you
drifting gently to sleep
dream of forever

"I've loved you, every day, since I first saw you,"

he yelled as she stormed out.

part three

it ended with rain

It was the kind of rain that falls noiselessly, just enough to know it's there. She stood cold and damp looking at the man that she was in love with. She didn't know how they had made it to this moment, but she wanted to be anywhere but standing in front of him, exchanging things left behind.

When she asked him to come outside, it seemed like she had so much to say, but now, facing the end of something she believed would be forever, she couldn't find the words. They stood in unsure silence, until he finally said what she already knew.

"I'm not in love with you," defeated, the words hung in the air as tears welled in her eyes.

She stared at her feet as he held onto his favorite sweatshirt, the one she'd slept in for the last six months. The silence dragged on as he reached out and gently pulled her in. She couldn't stop the tears, quietly sobbing into his shoulder, wrapping her arms around him and gripping the back of his jacket.

"I didn't want it to be like this," he said into her hair, choking on the words.

They stood like that for what seemed like a lifetime. Crying in the rain, no words left to say, but unable to say goodbye. She pulled back and looked up to wipe the tears from his face.

"I know," she said and she meant it. She had never felt as connected to anyone as she did to him, even in a short time, the love she had for him was something she wasn't likely to forget. The months that they had shared were some of the best of her life. He was her best friend. The memories of their time together came rushing in, she couldn't imagine getting in her car and never seeing him again. She touched his face and kissed his cheek, she looked deep into his clear blue eyes one last time, dropped her hand and took a step back.

"You know, just because I'm not your person, doesn't mean you aren't mine," she gave a half smile, took a deep breath, turned and walked to her car.

He didn't move. She got in, cranked the engine, wiped her tears, and without looking at him, backed out of the driveway. He stood there watching her go, until she turned the corner at the end of the street and lost sight of him in the rearview mirror.

when they ask
if I believe in soulmates
I'll smile softly
say ~~*no*~~
because I knew
long before it started
that you would have to go

I listen to that old voicemail
  on the nights that I can't sleep
    just one last time to hear you say

"thinking of you, I love you, wish I was there"

it doesn't stop the tears from falling
  it doesn't soften the ache
    that's made a hole in my chest
it does remind me of the time
  that I had you and it was real

a lesson they say
the way you loved then *pushed* away
I begged you to stay

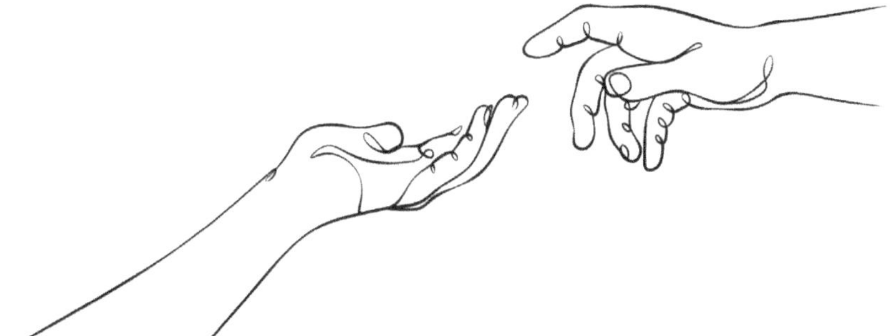

every time I hear your name
it cuts a little deeper
loving you washes over me
something like a fever
the tragedy of losing you
is that it *burned* you too
so here we are
two half souls
pretending to be whole

dazed in that place
between sleep and awake
your lazy footsteps
on the hardwood floor
never to be heard again
slipping into bed with me
a distant memory

I had it once
the love they write about
the kind that haunts dreams

I held it
held him

in the early morning hours
as the fire glowing sun
rose over rooftops
filtered in through the blinds

I had it once
felt it burn in my soul
it brought me to life
rose from the ashes

I held it
held him

like sand in my palm
slowly at first
then all at once
it was gone

I had it
had him
once

out of words to give
tears to fall and hearts to *grieve*
out of time to wait

I chose not to see
what was right in front of me
the subtle hints that you would *leave*
in the quiet way you loved me

after all this time
maybe we could try
the silence grows *louder*
time passes by
there are less days to miss you
even fewer to cry
on nights I want you most
I remind myself
I didn't build this wall
you could have called

memories
maybe just a *bad* dream
remnants of you and me
lost forgotten things
stuck on replay

pull me close
	I breathe you in
		fingertips trace my skin
echos in the dark
	go ahead
		leave your mark
run away
	rebuild those walls
		watch you lose it all
miss me
	like the sun in december
		something
you'll always remember

I tried to let go
to feel something new
the radio stopped *singing* about you
even though I can make it rhyme
watch the months slip by
it doesn't change what's true
I still...

I write love letters
burn them with the full moon
a ritual in learning
how to *forget* you

you on my mind
give it time
words never said
it's all in my head
I *hate* that it's still true
I wasn't done loving you

it's somehow always
also never
because together
it doesn't make sense

just like it's you
without me
everything is *tense*

in order to breathe
we needed space
one of us had to leave

the timing was wrong
the last words you said to me
not even *goodbye*

with my head screaming
it wasn't meant to be
my heart *shattering*
in too many fragments
        I let go

there are nights that I get so mad
as if I could talk myself out of feeling sad
then that first tear falls
the rest follow like they were called
to go to *war* for this burned out soul
I couldn't stop it from breaking apart
maybe they were all just lies
carefully hidden in sorrowful lines
the dreaded silence that comes
pretty distractions anything to numb
the thoughts that bring me back
to that night I know I was wearing black
cold air in my lungs as you opened the door
your eyes on me but I stared at the floor
one final exchange but not your heart for mine
the candles I'd left and a soft mumbled goodbye

maybe they're out there
maybe just as tired and worn down
on the verge of giving up
taking their love
packing it away too
maybe they're quietly waiting
maybe they'll fall in love
with the way you look at the world
in wide eyed wonder
maybe they'll hold your hand
it will feel just right
they'll kiss you goodnight
stars will shine *brighter*
maybe they're a little lost too
fighting to find you just the same
maybe

tell me everything
go ahead lay it out
how you can really see
everything that makes me

me

tell me once again
how it's not enough
break it down
like I don't know

say it

how you wish you felt it
it's better to be free
you don't love me

been burned too many times
to play with the fire
            put the matches away
            no time for desire
I've filled these pages
with everything
            except your name
            drowning in madness
of wanting your love
I gave up on your game

I have to skip that song when it starts to play
you sang it to me in the car
holding hands with all the windows down

do you remember?

I close my eyes and see it all so clearly
I can't watch that movie
you held me the whole time

do you remember?

we both cried in the dark because it made us feel alive
that night we sat outside and talked about the stars
you kissed my neck in front of the fire

do you remember?

I told you not to worry
that I would be okay
I kissed you one last time that day

do you remember?

you stood in the driveway
watching me go
I don't ever want to drive that road again

do you remember?

I wasn't what you wanted
even though I wished it wasn't true
you meant everything to me

do you remember?

About the Author

You can find me adventuring in Columbus, Ohio and chasing after my incredible, hilarious, and rambunctious three year old. I earned my BA in Creative Writing for Entertainment from Full Sail University, and have written everything from articles on mental health to fantasy stories about mermaids. My love of poetry stems from a deep yearning to validate the human experience and spectrum of emotions that we go through, especially when it comes to love. I write from a place of experience while drawing inspiration from the world around me.

Let's be Friends!
Instagram: @aeurbancreates
Twitter: @aeurbanwrites
Email: aeurbanwrites@gmail.com
Website: aeurbanwrites.wixsite.com/thetypewriterdiary

Other Titles:
Feeling Out Loud

"If guys don't want me to write bad songs about them,
they shouldn't do bad things."
- Taylor Swift (and Arianna Urban)

Acknowledgements

First I want to say a huge thank you to my friend Devon who has been an incredible support throughout my entire creative process in putting *when I believed in love* together. She read through it every step of the way while continuously cheering me on, thank you from the bottom of my heart. Kayley thank you for your kind words and for reading, re-reading, and then reading again.

Thank you to my family for the never ending encouragement. To everyone who has been reading my words since I was 17 and any new friends who bought this to read Anna's story, thank you for the unwavering love. I wouldn't have the courage to put my heart out into the world if it weren't for you. Thank you to R for the inspiration, your light, and bringing me back to myself, always. Yabbos, thank you for existing, for being the light in a very dark night, I love you to the end of the earth.